Twitter Decoded:
Tips & Tools for Authors

RUTH L. SNYDER

Creativity Press

ISBN: 0995229007
ISBN-13: 9780995229006

DISCLAIMER

The information and suggestions provided in this guide are based on resources that were current at the time the manual was written.

Social media and the World Wide Web are constantly changing and evolving. The author has done her best to provide accurate and current information along with helpful links. This information may change over time.

The author receives no compensation of any kind from Twitter and is not affiliated with Twitter in any way other than using a Twitter account.

Go to http://eepurl.com/Z9m7T to join Ruth's mailing list. You can find out more about the author and upcoming books at http://ruthlsnyder.com, and follow Ruth on Twitter http://www.twitter.com/wwjdr.

"The aim of marketing is to know and understand the customer so well the product or service fits him and sells itself."

—PETER DRUCKER

CONTENTS

CONTENTS (CONTINUED)

INTRODUCTION

I ventured into the virtual world of Twitter in 2009. As an upcoming writer, I knew I should be sharing my work on a broader scale by building my "platform." (A platform is a combination of tools an author uses to raise awareness of his message.) At that time, my five children were between the ages of one and eleven. When I told a fellow author that I didn't have time to be consistent with blogging, she encouraged me to try Twitter as a mini-blog.

Since then, as an author, I have used Twitter to share quotes from my articles and books, notify people when I write a new blog post, meet and interact with readers, other authors, publishers, and agents, ask for feedback, and even find information on topics I'm researching.

I managed to do all of this by spending an average of ten minutes or less a day on Twitter.

Authors are busy people. There are many expectations on us. Not only do we have to write our books or articles, but we are also expected to connect with our readers, other authors, publishers, etc. through various means, including social media.

If you're like me, you've discovered time mysteriously vanishes when you are on social media. How do we harness this monster so we can build and maintain those vital connections, and still get our writing done?

This book starts with the very basics for those who are not familiar with Twitter. I will share reasons to use Twitter and take you step-by-step through creating a Twitter account, updating a profile, and posting the first tweet.

After you are comfortable with Twitter basics, you will discover why and how to use hashtags, why and how to use link shorteners, easy steps to writing a great tweet, how to decide how often you should tweet, tools and sites to use with Twitter, why and how you should schedule your tweets, how to build relationships with tweeps (people on Twitter), and topics to tweet about. You will also find timesaving templates to use as you formulate your weekly tweets.

See you on Twitter!

CHAPTER 1 - GET TO KNOW TWITTER

Twitter (http://twitter.com) began in 2006 as a text message service that allowed members to communicate with a small group of contacts. Today, Twitter is one of many social media platforms available, with 233 million active users in 2013. [End Note 1] On Twitter you are able to post short (140 characters maximum) updates to share what you're doing or learning, link to interesting information, or ask questions. Twitter describes their service as:

" . . . a real-time information network that connects you to the latest information about what you find interesting. Simply find the public streams you find most compelling and follow the conversations . . . (Twitter is) like being delivered a newspaper whose headlines you'll always find interesting. Discover news as it's happening, learn more about topics that are important to you, and get the inside scoop . . ."

Benefits of Twitter

Writers are often scrambling to fit writing, education, and building a platform into their limited time. Why should writers use Twitter?

Tweets happen in real time.

Twitter allows you to both keep up with what's happening around you as well as share information immediately. If your book is released you can announce it immediately on Twitter. You don't have to wait until you have time to write a blog post or wait for the local newspaper to feature your book. You can provide a link to your book and post it on Twitter whenever you want.

Tweets encourage casual conversation.

Some marketers refer to Twitter as the "lounge" of marketing – a place where you can interact with people on an informal basis and develop relationships with them. It's a great place to network, find people with similar interests, and share information. Twitter also allows users to "retweet" or share something with their followers and reply to tweets others have posted. All of these features encourage conversations.

Twitter can be a great source of information for writers.

You can pose a question and ask people to RT (**retweet**). This gives you access to the opinions and knowledge of millions of people you may never meet in person. (In 2014, 115 million people used Twitter every month!) [End Note 2.]

Twitter enables you to build relationships with people all over the world.

This is true of other social media as well. As you build your list of followers, the people who follow your followers will also be exposed to the information you share. If you use **hashtags** (eg. #writers) effectively, you will be able to read and share information with people anywhere in the world who are interested in the same topics in which you are interested. (Hashtags are covered in more detail in Chapter 2. For now, get used to adding them to your tweets so that people will be able to find your information more easily.)

Twitter can help you build your platform.

Gary Mclaren says, "A platform is a foundation or base that someone has built that provides an opportunity for them to air their views publicly." [End Note 3] Not only can you get to know people, but you can also share information about books, share links to promotional items like coupons, and drive people to your website. I would caution you that Twitter works best when you see it as building a relationship — a two-way street: giving and receiving information. We all know what it's like when one person dominates the conversation at a party. After a while we get bored and move on. It's perfectly acceptable to use Twitter as a part of your marketing platform, but share what other people are saying too. A good rule of thumb is only use one tweet out of ten to promote yourself and your work. The other nine tweets should be replying to people, sharing information, and carrying on conversations. Michael Hyatt (@MichaelHyatt) says, "To be successful with Twitter, it can't be about you. It must be about your followers." [End Note 4]

Twitter can help generate sales.

This cannot be the only reason you use Twitter. However, if you develop a following of people who are interested in you and your products, Twitter can help generate sales. Minda Zetlin (@MindaZetlin) has some great tips in her post, "Launch a New Product on Twitter."

(http://www.inc.com/managing/articles/201006/twitter.html).

Your turn!

Go to www.Twitter.com/wwjdr and look around. Think about why and how you want to use Twitter. Use the search bar and type in a word or phrase to see what people are sharing about your favorite topic (Writing? Marketing? Fiction? Kindle? Etc.) Remember: Twitter is about building relationships, not about marketing per se.

RUTH L. SNYDER

CHAPTER 2 - YOUR USER NAME (HANDLE)

(http://ruthlsnyder.com/wp-content/uploads/2015/03/Twitter-Screen.png)

Your User Name (Handle)

Everyone who uses Twitter has a user name or handle (@wwjdr is mine). Choose your handle carefully, because your whole account is associated with it, and it is public. Many people use their names as their handle. I chose not to for two reasons. Firstly, Ruth Snyder is a common name and I wanted people to be able to find me easily. Secondly, I wanted a short handle so that when people retweeted me, my handle wasn't using up too many of those precious 140 characters. My handle stands for "What Would Jesus Do, Ruth?" Usernames may be up to 15 characters long. Twitter designates 20 characters for your real name. (On your Twitter account your real name will be shown first, followed by your handle.)

Your Bio

Your bio is one of the first things people look at when they are deciding whether they want to follow you or not. Another reason to choose your words wisely is that Google uses your bio as your Meta description for search engines. Brainstorm for a minute and jot down words that describe who you are and what you do. For example, if you specialize in the YA Genre, share that information. That's how your target audience (and fellow authors) will find you. Some of the words that describe me are married, mom, MYC teacher, President of ICWF, follower of Jesus, author. In my profile I've also let people know about some of my hobbies: reading, crafts, traveling, photography. If you have a website, make sure to include the link with your bio. Twitter only allows 160 characters in your bio. You'll receive an error message if you try to enter more.

> **TIP: Use *About Me* (http://about.me) and post the link in your Twitter profile. This enables you to share more information than if you just use the allotted 160 characters.**

Your turn!

1. Pick your Twitter Handle.
2. Brainstorm words that describe who you are and what you do, then put together your Twitter bio (160 characters max).
3. Ask someone you trust to look at your bio and provide feedback.

CHAPTER 3 - PREPARE A PROFILE PICTURE AND HEADER PICTURE

There's nothing that shouts "newbie" as loud as the "egghead" profile picture. With the technology we have now on cellphones and notebooks it's easy to snap a picture and upload it. Your profile picture will show up beside every tweet you share, so make sure it's an image you want people to remember. You can use a picture of yourself, a picture of your book cover, or maybe a picture of one of the characters from your story. Images must be JPG, GIF, or PNG files in order to upload them to Twitter.

> **TIP: Profile pictures should be 400 x 400 pixels. For more tips on Twitter pictures, check out Matt Silverman's** *5 Tips for Creating the Perfect Profile Pic.* **(http://mashable.com/2010/04/12/profile-picture-tips/)**

Your Header Picture

You can change the picture on your Twitter header. I've used different pictures here including scenery pictures and the cover photo from my latest book. Any time people click on your profile, they will see the header picture. You can develop your own header picture or use one offered by Twitter.

> **TIP: Twitter recommends header pictures sized at 1500 x 500 pixels. Check out** *The New Twitter Header Dimensions & Template Included.*
>
> (http://www.twelveskip.com/tutorials/twitter/1267/twitter-header-size-dimension-2014.)
>
> **Both** Canva **and** PicMonkey **are free online picture editors which provide pre-sized Twitter header options.**

Your Turn!

1. Watch the Youtube Video about updating your profile and header photos. (https://youtu.be/J79Ek7gezw0).
2. Figure out what you're going to use for each picture.

CHAPTER 4 - SET UP YOUR TWITTER ACCOUNT

Now that you've figured out the first steps, it's time to set up your account at www.Twitter.com.

1. Enter your full name (as you want it to appear on Twitter), a valid e-mail address, and a password. Then click on "Sign up for Twitter."

2. Check to make sure the information is correct. Enter the user name or handle you chose in Chapter 2 and click "Sign Up." You'll have to wait for Twitter to e-mail a confirmation that your account is set up before you proceed.

3. After you receive the confirmation e-mail, go to www.Twitter.com and log in with your user name and password.

Your Turn!

Make sure you can log in to your account before moving to Chapter 5. You may want to work your way through Getting Started with Twitter (https://support.twitter.com/articles/215585#). It includes many tips, shared by the people who created and developed the platform.

CHAPTER 5 - UPDATING YOUR PROFILE

When you open a Twitter account, the profile is very basic and plain. You need to update this as soon as possible to remove that egghead and let people know who you really are. You'll find the profile menu in the top right hand corner of your screen. Click on "View profile," right under your name. (On mobile devices, click on your picture to reveal the menu, and select "Profile".

To update your profile, click on "Edit profile":

You can now update your profile picture, header, name, bio, location, website link, and theme colours. Don't forget to click "Save changes" when you're done.

(http://ruthlsnyder.com/wp-content/uploads/2015/03/Updating-Profile.png)

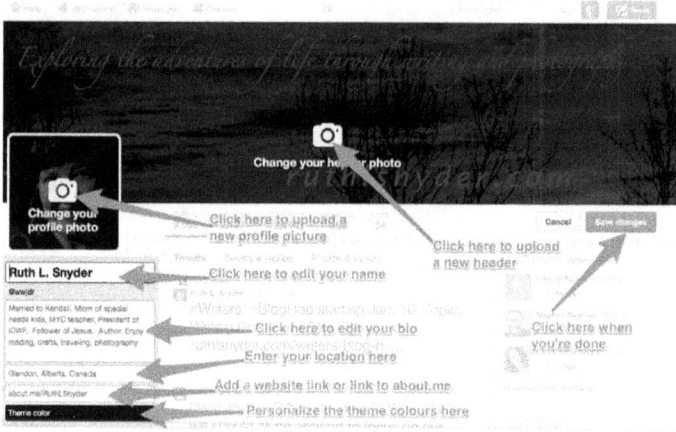

Your Turn!

1. Check out some other people's profiles and make note of what you like or don't like.

2. Update your own profile.

CHAPTER 6 - YOUR FIRST TWEET

When you start out using Twitter, you may want to lurk for a while — just spend time reading what other people say and share. When you're ready to tweet, here are some suggestions:

1. Be original, useful, authentic, witty and helpful.
2. Share links to information you've found helpful (a news item, software tool, or blog post).
3. Offer advice on how to do things, how NOT to do things, what people should avoid etc.
4. Ask questions. Michael Hyatt (@MichaelHyatt) suggests: "Use the 'wisdom of crowds' to do everything from finding a great restaurant to solving a specific problem."
5. Tweet when you post a book review.
6. Teach something you've learned about writing.
7. Share a recent blog post. (You can also link your blog to Twitter. One way to do this is by using Twitterfeed.com.
8. Invite people to a book signing.
9. Announce a book launch.
10. Provide a discount code with a link for followers to purchase your book.
11. Give away a free copy of your book to people who tweet or

post about it on Facebook. (Use Pay with a Tweet
http://www.paywithatweet.com/.

12. Congratulate others on achievements.
13. Share a picture 15+ Tools to Send, Upload or Share Files on
    Twitter http://www.aboutonlinetips.com/how-to-send-files-
    on-twitter/. Brittany Leaning (@bleaning) says, "Since we
    started using photos in tweets along with a short URL . . .
    we've seen the average conversion rate on those pages nearly
    double."
14. Promote a contest you're hosting on your blog.
15. Share a quote from a favorite author.
16. Tweet quotes from your latest book.
17. Share what you're learning at a writer's conference.
18. Share good reviews you receive.
19. Tweet a review of a product or book you like.

From the "Home" screen, you can click on the "What's
happening" space and enter your tweet.

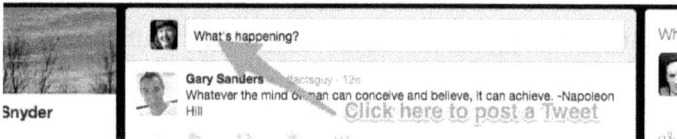

**Tip: You don't always have to be sitting at your
computer to use Twitter. Download a Twitter app
(https://twitter.com/download) to use on your smart
phone. You can also use TwitterMail
(http://twittercounter.com/pages/twittermail) or Big
Big Tweet (http://www.bigbigtweet.com/) to post
longer tweets.**

If you're on your profile screen, click on the "Tweet" button in
the top right hand corner to enter your tweet. (See image on the next
page).

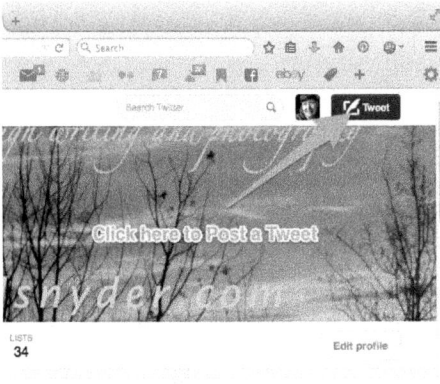

Your Turn!

Post your first tweet!

CHAPTER 7 - FOLLOWING TWEEPS (PEOPLE ON TWITTER)

Twitter is like anything else that's worthwhile—it takes time, consistency, and hard work. Remember, you want to use Twitter to build relationships. Dr. Sarah Eaton (@DrSarahEaton) says, "You don't need more followers. You want more **engaged** followers."

When you choose to follow someone on Twitter, you're subscribing to his or her tweets. There are several ways to find interesting people to follow.

1. Type names of high profile authors or other people in the writing industry into the search bar to find their Twitter handle.   Then select their account and click "follow". (http://ruthlsnyder.com/wp-content/uploads/2015/03/Follow.png)

2. Click on the "following" and "followers" lists of people you're following to find more people you may want to follow. (http://ruthlsnyder.com/wp-cotent/uploads/2015/03/Following.png)

3. Type generic words like writer, author, agent, publisher, etc. into the search bar to find others who have interests similar to your own.

(http://ruthlsnyder.com/wp-content/uploads/2015/03/Search.png)

4. Read the Twitter feed (all the entries on your Twitter account) and follow people who have tweets that are interesting to you.

5. Import your email contacts (https://support.twitter.com/articles/101002#)

6. Check out suggestions from Twitter (Click on the #Discover menu and select "Who to follow" or "Popular accounts" in the top right column.) (http://ruthlsnyder.com/wp-content/uploads/2015/03/Discover.png)

7. Twellow.com and Twibes.com are helpful tools to find people in your niche. Most people will follow you back when you follow them.

> **Tip: Make sure you only follow people you care about. Also, be careful not to follow more than a couple hundred people per day; otherwise the Twitter spam team may suspend your account.**

Your Turn!

Find 100 interesting people and follow them.

CHAPTER 8 - BE CAREFUL!

A Word of Caution

Twitter has a dark side too. Before you follow someone, check out his or her profile. If the person's bio or picture is non-existent, the person has no tweets, the person has no followers, the bio makes you feel uncomfortable, or the profile picture is questionable, DO NOT follow them. You are able to block and/or report people on Twitter. Check out Twitter's suggestions about offensive content: (https://support.twitter.com/articles/20170133#).

There are services that sell Twitter followers. Don't buy followers; instead, build your own organic following. (When you build your list of followers yourself, you build relationships and establish trust.)

Things You Should NOT Do on Twitter

1. **DON'T Type in all capitals** – Those who interact on other social media sites know that typing in all capitals is like yelling.

2. **DON'T Tweet when you're angry** – Never say anything on Twitter that you would be ashamed to see on

the front page of a newspaper. If you're angry, it's better not to tweet than to wish you hadn't. Take some time to cool off so that you're thinking logically and won't live to regret your tweets.

3. **DON'T Repeat tweets too often** – This is something you may have to experiment with a bit. There's nothing wrong with repeating tweets at different times of day so a different audience sees your message. However, if you repeat tweets too often you may lose some of your followers.

4. **DON'T Retweet all the time** – Retweeting is fine, but you need to provide your own content too. Otherwise, people may wonder if you're able to think for yourself.

5. **DON'T Post third party tweets** – Many games and services request permission to post on your behalf. These tweets can be annoying, like spam, and may result in you losing followers.

6. **DON'T Use automatic Direct Messages to make sales** – There are services (e.g. SocialOomph, TwitterDMer and TweetManager) that will send out automatic direct messages to people when they follow you. It's fine to send people a welcome message like, "Thanks for following me, I look forward to getting to know you better," but don't use your welcome message to ask for a sale.

Your Turn!

Check out Twitter's suggestions for safe tweeting: (https://support.twitter.com/articles/76036#

CHAPTER 9 - CRAFTING GREAT TWEETS

What makes a good tweet? The answer to this question will differ somewhat based on what your goals are for Twitter. You can find tips by Googling "What Makes a Good Tweet," but here are some questions to consider:

1. Who is your target audience?
2. What type of information is your audience looking for? What will pique their attention?
3. Which Twitter users would be interested in your tweet? (Alexis Grant (@alexisgrant) suggests 90% of tweets should contain a mention, which means you include the person's Twitter handle in your tweet.)
4. What time of day is your audience most likely to see your tweet? (You'll learn this by trial and error.)
5. Is there a helpful link you can share? (Twitter has its own link shortner, but you may want to use Bit.ly or a similar shortener so that you can track which links are most effective.)
6. Would I enjoy reading this if someone else wrote it?

TIP: If you post a tweet with an error in it, you are able to delete your tweet. However, you need to

remember that once something is live on the internet, there may be a permanent record of it. (Some people call this "making cement footprints.") You may delete your tweet, but someone else may have copied it and passed it on or placed it into a different format where you can't access it. So be sure that what you post is what you really want to say.

(http://ruthlsnyder.com/wp-content/uploads/2015/03/Twitter-delete.png)

Your Turn!

Check out more helpful tips at Good Tweet vs. Bad Tweet: A Guide to Being Not Boring on Twitter.
(http://slidesha.re/1eOVX1W)

CHAPTER 10 - BUILDING RELATIONSHIPS ON TWITTER

It's one thing to follow someone on Twitter. However, in order to use Twitter effectively, you need to interact with people. Replying allows you to "carry on a conversation." Clicking "Favorite" lets people know that you like what they are sharing. (It's also a great way to mark tweets you want to go back to later.)
(http://ruthlsnyder.com/wp-content/uploads/2015/03/Favourite1.png)

Replying

The easiest way to reply to a person on Twitter is to use his or her handle (like "@wwjdr What do you think of this idea?") in your tweet. You can click on the "reply" icon at the bottom of the tweet.

You can also retweet or repeat what someone else tweeted by clicking on the retweet icon at the bottom of the tweet (between the reply and favorite icon). When you retweet something, that information is posted on the Twitter feed again, so the more something is retweeted by multiple people, the more likely that others will see it. When you do retweet, add a comment as well.

Favorites

When you like something you see on Twitter, you can indicate you like the tweet by clicking on the Favorite icon (star). When you click on favorite, the tweet is saved and you can access it any time by clicking on the Favorites menu.

Your Turn!

1. Reply to some tweets and see if you can start a conversation.
2. Scroll through current tweets or search a topic you're interested in and favorite some tweets.

CHAPTER 11 - HASHTAGS

What are Hashtags?

A hashtag is a pound sign (#) followed by any word(s), used to categorize messages (e.g. #ebook or #quote or #TheArtofWorkBook)

How to use Hashtags

If you click on any hashtag, all the tweets using that hashtag will show up. (You can also use the search feature to find tweets on any topic/hashtag.)

http://ruthlsnyder.com/wp-content/uploads/2015/06/Hashtag.png

Hashtag(s) may be placed anywhere in your tweet. Although you are able to use as many hashtags in a tweet as you want, most people recommend using only one to three per tweet. Check out popular hashtags for writers below.

As part of your marketing platform, you probably want to create your own hashtag related to a book or one of your other products. Use the search feature to make sure the hashtag is not being used by someone else. Some other tools you can use are TwiTag.com, Twubs.com, and Hashtags.org. Remember that you only have 140 characters to work with for each tweet, so keep your hashtags as short as possible. However, a hashtag also needs to be long enough to make sense. For instance, when Jeff Goins (@JeffGoins) published his *The Art of Work* book, he chose #TheArtofWorkBook as the hashtag. He could have left the words "the and "book" off, but the words clarify what the tweets are about. Using something like #AoWB wouldn't mean anything to most people.

For this book, I've registered #TwitterDecodedForAuthors on Twubs.com.

Popular hashtags for writers

#amediting (posts from people who are editing)
#amwriting (information about something you're writing)
#askagent (agent questions & answers)
#author

#authors
#editing
#ebook
#editmark
#editmongering (word "sprints" that happen every ½ hour for 30 min.)
#epublish
#fictionfriday
#fridayflash (flash fiction on a Friday)
#NaNoWriMo (national novel writing month)
#novels (Share your novel's front cover)
#novelists (Inspirational pictures and quotes for novelists)
#poem
#poet
#poets
#poetry
#pubtip (publication tips)
#publishing
#quote
#reader (a good place to recommend books to readers)
#reading (let your friends and followers know what you're reading)
#SciFi
#selfpublishing
#shelfster (Shelfster.com)
#vss (very short story)
#webfic (web fiction)
#weblit (web literature)
#wip (work in progress)
#wordcount
#wordmongering (similar to word "sprints" that happen every ½ hour for 30 minutes)
#writegoal
#writequote
#writer
#writers
#writetip (writing advice)
#writetips
#writing
#writingtips

#wrotetoday

For even more hashtag ideas, read *Hashtags for Every Day of the Week #Hashtags* by **John Kremer (@JohnKremer)**
(http://bookmarketingbestsellers.com/hashtags-for-every-day-of-the-week-hashtags/)

Your Turn!

1. Read through the list of hashtags again and choose two hashtags to use in your tweets this week.
2. If you don't know which hashtags to pick, try #amwriting (it will motivate you to keep writing so you have something new to tweet about) and #quote (share your favourite quotes about writing and/or share some quotes from your current work in progress to pique people's attention and build some hype).
3. This week when you sign into your Twitter account, spend a few minutes reading some tweets that show up under one of the above hashtags. This will help you become familiar with the types of tweets posted under each hashtag and help you know which hashtag(s) to use when you want to reach a particular audience on Twitter.
4. If you are working on writing a book, or have books published, spend a few minutes doing some research on hashtags. Select a unique hashtag to use for marketing your book.

Want more suggestions? Check out *How Twitter and Hashtags Can Help Your PR and Marketing:*
http://www.marketwired.com/howtwitterandhashtags.pdf.

CHAPTER 12 – LINK SHORTENERS

Since Twitter limits tweets to 140 characters (except for Direct Messages), you want to make the best use of each one. (NOTE: As of May 2016, Twitter no longer includes Twitter handles and images in the character limit. http://money.cnn.com/2016/05/24/technology/twitter-character-limit/index.html) Links are often long, using precious characters you could be using for other purposes. That's why you should become familiar with link shorteners, which allow you to paste a long link into them and magically present you with a short link which still takes people to the website designated in the link. Bit.do lists shorteners available. (http://bit.do/list-of-url-shorteners.php) You do not have to have a shortener account to use one. These shorteners are provided free of charge.

Twitter actually has its own link shortener, t.co, which will automatically shorten any link you place in a tweet. However, you will have no way of tracking how effective your links are. http://ruthlsnyder.com/wp-content/uploads/2015/06/t-co.png

Other shorteners specific to particular software or apps include lnkd.in (for LinkedIn), db.tt (for Dropbox), qr.ae (for Quora) goo.gl (for Google), and cur.lv (for Bitcoin). You can choose to use only one shortener service, or use several of them.

The link shortener I've used and seen used the most is bit.ly:

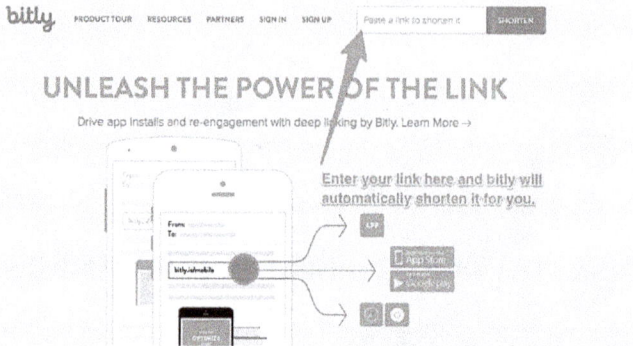

Although you can use bit.ly without opening an account, there is no advantage to using bit.ly instead of t.co if you don't have an account. Bit.ly provides useful analytics that will help you in your marketing efforts.

Here's how you create a bit.ly account:

1. Go to https://bitly.com/. Click on "Sign Up."

2. Sign up by creating an account rather than signing up with Facebook or Twitter.

   Tip: the bit.ly sidebar makes it easier to find content and share short links.

3. Sign into your account.

4. Copy the link you want shortened (e.g. My Book) and paste it into the bit.ly link shortener.

   TIP: You can use the automatic link bit.ly gives you, or you can customize it by clicking on the pencil icon (edit) and giving it a name you choose.

5. Copy the shortened link by clicking on "copy".

Bitly Link Shortener

http://amzn.to/1ewcGuf

DONE! YOU'VE CREATED YOUR BITLINK

http://amzn.to/1ewcGuf
amazon.com/Learn-Twitter-Beginning-Authors-Mastery-ebook/dp/B00VFETELG/ref=sr_1_1?ie=U...

6. Share the link wherever you want – social media and/or e-mail.

7. Go back to your bit.ly account to receive detailed information on how your link is performing. (see next page for an example)

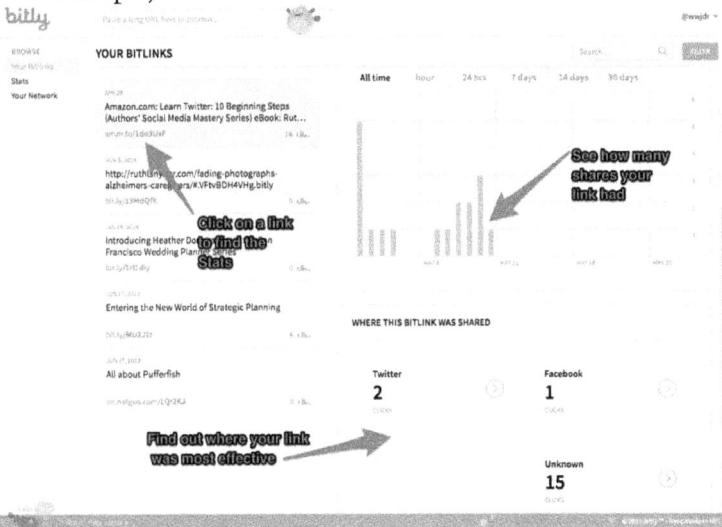

Your Turn!

1. Sign up with Bit.ly.
2. Create a Bit.ly link and share it on social media and/or e-mail.
3. Go back to your Bit.ly account to receive detailed information on how your link is performing.

RUTH L. SNYDER

CHAPTER 13 - THREE EASY STEPS
TO CREATING GREAT TWEETS

Writing effective tweets can be a challenge. However, there are several things you can do that will make your job easier.

Choose your topic/content

Remember that although your goal may be sales, your focus needs to be on building relationships. Put yourself in your follower's (prospective customer's) shoes:

What topics is he interested in?

What is her felt need?

What problem does he want resolved?

What makes her laugh? Or cry?

According to **Dave Larson (@TweetSmarter)**, the types of tweets which receive the most engagement are warnings, quotes, trending news, fun quizzes, summaries, tips, and resources. Pictures also increase the chances of your tweet receiving attention.

Shea Bennett (@Sheamus) states only two things count on Twitter: readability and retweetability. He urges that we learn how to differentiate between selling links and selling content:

"…the content is what will sell your product or idea, but nobody is going to care about any of that unless you've first sold them the reason to read it. You might have discovered the cure for cancer, but nobody is going to care if you link it next to 'This is cool'."

Summarize the topic/information

Summarizing your main point is similar to writing a catchy headline. **Jeff Goins** (@JeffGoins) says, "Too often the headline is the most neglected part… People just gloss over it without taking much time to consider it. In their minds, it's the cherry on top. No, friends; it's not. The headline is the sundae." He shares this formula: Number or Trigger word + adjective + keyword + promise.

Add a graphic or link

If you're sharing a quote, a graphic will garner more attention.

Donna Moritz (@SociallySorted) has an informative infographic about the Importance of visual content at http://graphs.net/importance-of-visual-content-on-social-media.html

Michael Stelzner of Social Media Examiner (@smexaminer) says,

"When you **merge the power of imagery with original content**, then it gets shared a lot. If you can create some of your own original content, you've got more chance of it being shared, versus having to share everybody else's. It's very powerful."

If you need more convincing, read How to Use Images to Skyrocket Your Blog Traffic: A Case Study of 100 Million Articles at http://snip.ly/Dbcz.

My favorite apps for creating graphics are WordSwag for iPhone or iPad, Canva.com, and PicMonkey.com. You can watch my video about creating beautiful graphics on PicMonkey at https://youtu.be/bwZLqsnAoHQ.) We've already discussed how to obtain shortened links using bit.ly.

Writing good tweets takes some practice, so be patient with yourself. Try different formats and topics and see what works best with your audience.

Your turn!

Create 5 tweets using the steps outlined in this chapter.

1. Choose a topic
2. Summarize the topic (aim for 80-90 words)
3. Add your link
4. Add an eye-catching graphic

Put all that together and post your tweets. Pay attention to which tweets get the most retweets, favorites, conversations, and mentions, and write more tweets like those. You may also want to pay attention when you're reading other people's tweets. Which ones do you disregard? Why? Which ones do you pay attention to and comment on, favorite, or retweet? Why? This will give you vital information you can put to use when creating your own tweets.

In chapter 16, we'll be discussing scheduling your tweets. Once you know which tweets work best, it will be easier to decide which ones to schedule.

RUTH L. SNYDER

CHAPTER 14 - HOW OFTEN SHOULD YOU TWEET?

How often should you tweet? The answer to this question varies depending on who you ask. Some people say you should only tweet a few times a day, and always spread your tweets out. Others flood Twitter with tweets.

Guy Kawasaki (@GuyKawasaki), author of *APE: Author, Publisher, Entrepreneur – How to Publish a Book* has 1.4 million followers. He makes it a habit to schedule 50 different tweets each day and repeats each of those 50 tweets four times, or every eight hours.

There are also a variety of opinions about the appropriate balance between promoting yourself and providing valuable content.

Joe Pulizzi (@JoePulizzi), founder of the Content Marketing Institute popularized the 4-1-1 rule: For every "self-serving" tweet, make sure you retweet someone else's tweet and then share four pieces of pertinent content that will be interesting and helpful to your followers.

> **TIP: Make sure you check out links and resources BEFORE you retweet them. Sometimes links are broken, or the information isn't what you're led to**

believe. When your tweets and retweets are always reliable, people will trust you.

Grant Cardone (@GrantCardone) says,

"There is no such thing as posting too much content . . . Those who quit following you because you post too much aren't your market and won't buy from you anyway. If people aren't complaining about how much you post you are not posting enough."

Grant suggests that 80% - 95% of your content should be information and only 5% - 20% should be promotional.

Your turn!

1. Assess what you're currently posting on Twitter:
   - How many tweets per day or week?
   - How many informational/general tweets compared to promotional tweets?
   - What do you want to tweak or change?
2. Read *How to Write a Marketing Plan for Twitter* (http://tweakyourbiz.com/marketing/2011/02/18/how-to-write-a-marketing-plan-for-twitter/) by Ivan Walsh (@ivanwalsh)
3. Create your own marketing plan for Twitter.

CHAPTER 15 - TOOLS AND SITES TO USE WITH TWITTER

Obviously, if you're going to tweet throughout the day on a regular basis AND get your writing done, you'll need tools to help you. Many services have a free version. Some tools allow you to schedule and share content. Other tools will help you find great content to share. Here are a few suggestions:

Alltop.com

Alltop is a great way to find content to share on Twitter. It provides links to popular stories from many different platforms including New York Times, Forbes, USA Today, Tech Meme, Wikimedia picture of the day, Reuters most popular video, and many more.

Buffer.com

Buffer allows you to use a browser extension (available for Chrome, Safari, or Firefox) to collect content and send it out well distributed throughout the day. This is a great app to use if you don't want to overwhelm people with your tweets. You can spend a focused time during the day gathering content and Buffer will spread the tweets out over the day. Buffer will work on multiple accounts and will buffer RTs on Twitter.com. (Buffer also has a Pinterest app.)

Commun.it

Want to build your Twitter tribe? Communi.it not only reveals all your followers, but also orders them so that you can see who is most engaged, who really supports you, and who your influencers are. This app will also show mentions of your blog or brand that are made outside your network.

Feedly.com

Do you find yourself "hopping" all over the internet trying to find great content to share? Feedly gives you one location to read your favorite newspapers, magazines, and blogs. First you personalize the app by selecting sources of information you want to include. Then you can access Feedly from the web, an iOS, or Android device and read to find great content.

Hootsuite.com

Are you looking for a dashboard where you can manage your social media? Hootsuite works with Twitter, Facebook, Google+ Instagram, Youtube, LinkedIn and thirty other social networks.
You are able to schedule messages, interact with your audience and check ROI from the Hootsuite dashboard. The personal version is free, or you can pay for the small business option or large corporation account.

IFTTT.com

IFTTT allows you to make connections between anything you do online. It gives you two "Recipe" options. A "Do Recipe" will perform a function like uploading photos to an album or posting an event onto your calendar. An "IF Recipe" helps create connections between apps and sites. For instance you can make a recipe that states you want all the pictures you post on Instagram to be saved to your Dropbox. This app allows you to be creative in linking totally unrelated apps.

JustRetweet.com

This is an app to use if you are a blogger and want to increase your reach across social media platforms like Facebook and Google+. "You not only get more exposure to your content, but will also likely gain new Twitter followers as a result."

ManageFlitter.com

Is it time to clean up your Twitter account? Try ManageFlitter. This app shows you who is not following back, and which accounts are not active any more. No account is necessary. Once on ManageFlitter you just click on the "Sign In" tab and then click "Connect to Twitter" to log into your Twitter account.

Pinterest.com

Are you a visual person? Pinterest is like a giant virtual corkboard where you can find information and "pin" it to your own board. This is a great place to find and save useful content. You can type any word or combination of words into the search. Fair warning: this is an easy place to waste time!

Seesmic (http://seesmic-desktop.en.softonic.com)

Seesmic is a desktop app similar to Hootsuite and Tweetdeck which allows you to interact with various social media sites like Twitter, Facebook, LinkedIn, MySpace, Ning, Formspring, Last.fm and YouTube. Some people say the app is easy to use, but clunky.

StumbleUpon.com

Want a quick, easy way to access great content? Try StumbeUpon. You can either connect using Facebook or sign up for a free account. Once you open the app, you're able to specify the topics you're interested in and add them to any collection you want to create. For instance, my interests are arts, crafts, music, photography, travel, books, family, nature, and quotes. I can ask StumbleUpon to show everything pertaining to my interests ("All Interests"), ("Activity"), or select "what's trending", "photos", or "videos".

TweetDeck (http://tweetdeck.twitter.com

If you want to see everything that's happening related to your account on Twitter in one dashboard, try TweetDeck. It allows you to organize and build collections according to your likes and tastes. You can keep track of lists, searches, and other activity. TweetDeck also allows you to search topics, events, and hashtags and filter them.

You may use multiple accounts on TweetDeck. I've tried TweetDeck, but find the constantly updating screens overwhelming.

Tweriod.com

Tweriod is a free app that analyses your tweets and your followers' tweets and lets you know when your tweets will get the most exposure.

Your Turn!

Choose one tool from the above list (if you don't know where to start, try Pinterest) and try it out this week. Perhaps you want to try a new one every week until you've tried them all. Then, figure out which tools help you and use those tools.

CHAPTER 16 - SCHEDULING YOUR TWEETS

Why would an author want to schedule tweets? So that you can be active on Twitter, but also get your writing done! Preparing tweets for a week or more will take a half hour or so once a week, but by doing this, the ten or fifteen minutes you spend on Twitter every day will give you the opportunity to interact with your followers and build stronger connections.

Figure out how many tweets you want to schedule each day and what you want to tweet about and then you can draw up a schedule and enter the tweets into one of the apps. (Pick one from the previous chapter, if you haven't already.)

(**Chris Robley** (@chrisrobley) has a suggested schedule for two writing related tweets a day on his blog post *How to Promote Your Book on Twitter: An Intermediate's Guide to Tweeting:* (http://blog.bookbaby.com/2012/12/twitter-202-for-authors-an-intermediates-guide-to-promoting-your-book-with-tweets/). If you want to write your own marketing plan for Twitter, purchase my Social Media Marketing package from http://ruthlsnyder.com.

Choose one day to enter all the tweets for a week. (If possible, stick to one day consistently so that this becomes a habit.)

Then, make sure you check in every day to comment, reply, and carry on conversations with people who've responded to your tweets. (Your daily check in is the topic of the next chapter.)

Your Turn!

1. Write and schedule tweets for one full week, based on your Twitter marketing plan.

   I personally prefer Hootsuite for scheduling my tweets.

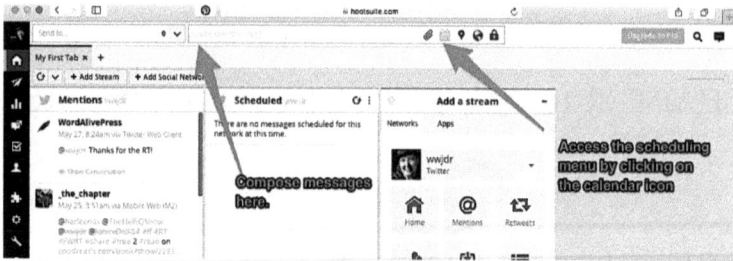

2. Enter your tweets (assuming you're scheduling to Twitter) in the top bar "Compose..." Click on the little calendar icon to schedule your tweets.

   TIP: You have the option to tell Hootsuite when to schedule the tweet OR you can allow Hootsuite to decide ("Autoschedule").

CHAPTER 17 - NOTIFICATIONS, TRENDS AND MENTIONS

Building relationships on Twitter works in many of the same ways as building relationships face to face. Learn to listen. Spend time with people by having two-way conversations. Make sure you discuss topics that are mutually interesting and avoid focusing on yourself.

Twitter has some features that are helpful in building relationships: Notifications, Trends and Mentions.

http://ruthlsnyder.com/wp-content/uploads/2015/06/Notifications-and-Trends.png

About Notifications:

Click on Notifications to see who followed you, who retweeted you, and who favorited your tweets.

http://ruthlsnyder.com/wp-content/uploads/2015/06/Notifications.png

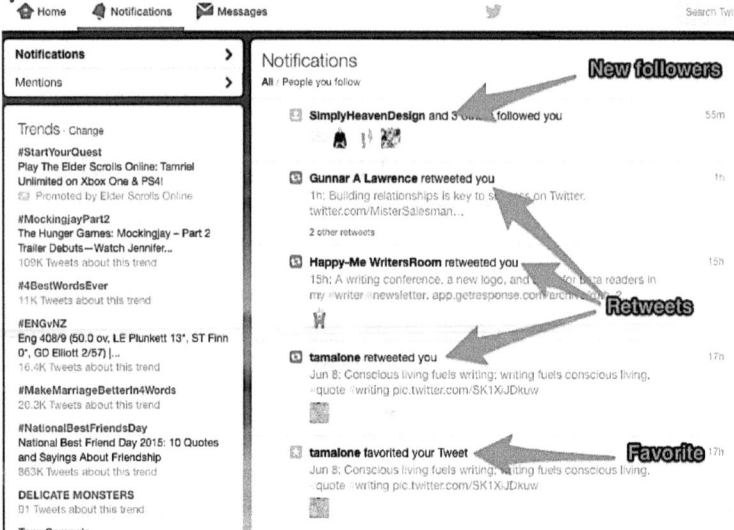

Click on the small image of each person who followed you to see his/her profile.

http://ruthlsnyder.com/wp-content/uploads/2015/06/New-followers.png

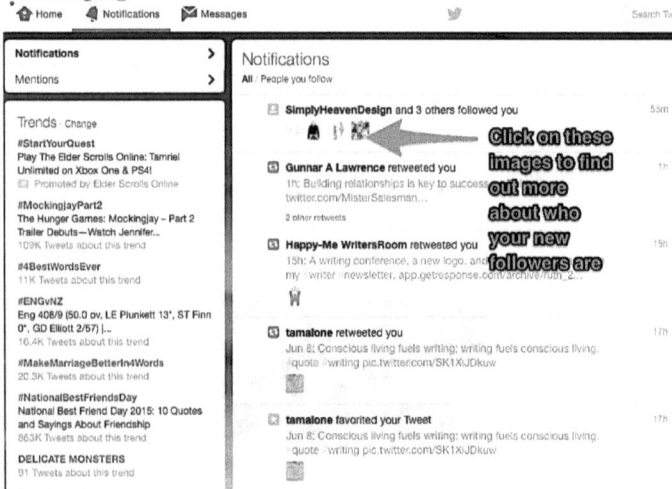

Take a look at each profile to decide whether you want to follow back or not.

http://ruthlsnyder.com/wp-content/uploads/2015/06/New-followers.png

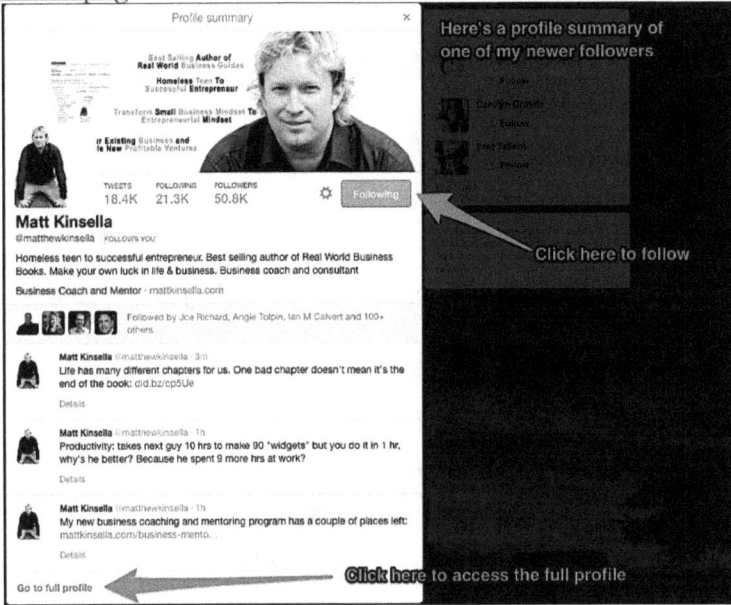

When you're done, click on the "x" in the top right hand corner to close the profile summary.

About Mentions

Mentions let you know when someone is talking about you, or asking you a question, or maybe even alerting you to some information.
http://ruthlsnyder.com/wp-content/uploads/2015/06/Mentions.png

Here (see link below and picture on the next page) are some details from mentions I received. You'll see that I've been carrying on a conversation with Joy. The Besty Travelers is asking me a question. Anne is suggesting other people may be interested in following me. http://ruthlsnyder.com/wp-content/uploads/2015/06/Mention-details.png

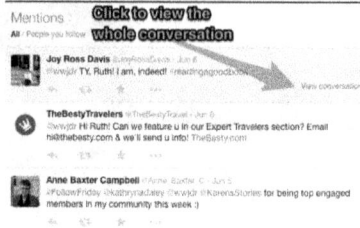

Here's the conversation between Joy and I. http://ruthlsnyder.com/wp-content/uploads/2015/06/Conversation-sample.png

About Trends

Trends will keep you aware of what topics are trending on Twitter and make it easier to figure out what conversations you may want to join. (See next page for graphic.)
http://ruthlsnyder.com/wp-content/uploads/2015/06/Trending-Topics.png

Here's a sample from the Trending topic #4BestWordsEver
http://ruthlsnyder.com/wp-
content/uploads/2015/06/Tweets_about__4BestWordsEver_hashta
g_on_Twitter.png

Your turn!

Spend a few minutes each day building relationships with people on Twitter.

1. Go to notifications and find your new followers. Read their bios, check out some of their tweets, and follow those you want to follow.
2. Check out the recent retweets and favorites and thank these people.
3. Go to mentions and interact with your friends.
4. Check trending topics to see which ones interest you and

would be useful to your followers.

5. Remember that relationship building takes time and consistency. Have fun!

CHAPTER 18 - SMART TOPICS FOR WRITERS TO TWEET ABOUT

Are you stumped when it comes to deciding what to tweet about? We've already discussed that you need to tweet about things your individual audience is interested in, but there are some general topics any writer can tweet about.

Sandi Krakowski (@sandikrakowski) suggests:
- Pictures of flowers
- Link to a favorite recipe
- Fun questions (What's your favorite flavor of ice-cream? What's the best book you've ever read? If you could be any cartoon character, who would you be? Who's your hero?)
- Inspiring quotes
- Things that make people laugh

Pam Moore (@PamMktgNut) shares 100 ideas to tweet about http://www.pammarketingnut.com/2013/03/100-things-to-tweet-about-on-twitter-besides-yourself/ including:

- Tips to help people save money
- Photos of you that show your human side
- How-to tips
- Jokes
- Pictures of nature
- Thank a favorite writer or blogger
- Link to a favorite song
- Ask a thought-provoking question
- Tweet a whole story
- Share when you reach a goal
- Share a daily thought
- Tweet a positive review you received

Jenn Hanson-dePaula (@Jenndepaula) shares 40 ideas at https://twitter.com/Jenndepaula such as:
- Mention (@[Twitter Handle]) one of your fans, thanking them for supporting you
- Share an old picture for #TBT (Throw Back Thursday)
- Write a Haiku
- Share something that has helped you in your writing
- Share the title of a book you're reading and mention the author

Your turn!

Use one new idea each day this week in your Tweets. At the end of the week, use your "Notifications" and your bit.ly links to track which tweets get the most response and continue to use those ideas.

CHAPTER 19 - TWEET TEMPLATES FOR WRITERS

Tweet templates can save you time and still provide your audience with a variety of interesting tweets. You will want to use evergreen tweets to build your template. "Evergreen" tweets are those you can use over and over again, as long as you only repeat them occasionally. Your evergreen tweets could include promotional posts for books or other products you have available for sale, quotes, review snippets with a link to your sales page, and tips related to your genre or books.

Shelley Hitz (@shelleyhitz) suggests you post tweets a minimum of at least once each day so that you'll have 365 tweets in a year. You may want to try using IFTTT.com to download the tweets you've already posted. After you delete time sensitive tweets, you'll have a good start on a file of posts to use for years to come. This will become your twitter template.

Kimberley Payne (@FitforFaith) compiled quotes with 140 characters or less which are great to use on Twitter. You can download the quotes from http://ruthlsnyder.com/wp-content/uploads/2015/07/Quotes-to-use-on-Twitter.pdf and add them to your templates.

Lindsay Kolowich (@lkolo25) provides some helpful templates in her blog post, How to Tweet on Twitter: *12 Templates to Get You*

Started: http://blog.hubspot.com/marketing/tweet-formulas-to-get-you-started-on-twitter. You can simply personalize the templates and add them to your evergreen list.

> **TIP: You can obtain a copy of all your tweets from Twitter. Sign into your account. Click on Settings. Choose Account. Scan down and click on "Request your archive". Twitter will e-mail you with a link to your file.**

Your turn!

Put together your own template of tweets. You could create 365 evergreen tweets or start with 30 tweets you can reuse every month.

CHAPTER 20 - SUMMING IT UP

In this book you've learned how to set up and update your Twitter account, compose effective tweets, use Twitter tools to find content and share your tweets, build relationships with other tweeps, and put together evergreen tweets.

You are now equipped to use Twitter effectively!

- Follow me (@wwjdr) and I'll see you on Twitter!
- Join my private Facebook group (Learn Twitter https://www.facebook.com/groups/LearnTwitterGroup/) to share ideas on how to use Twitter most effectively.
- Connect with me on my website at http://ruthlsnyder.com.

If you found this book helpful, I would be thankful for a review on Amazon and Goodreads. Please also tell your friends about *Twitter Decoded*. Thanks!

END NOTES

1. http://www.mediabistro.com/alltwitter/twitter-active-users-growth_b50145

2. http://www.statisticbrain.com/twitter-statistics/

3. http://www.platformpundit.com/what-is-a-marketing-platform/

TWITTER GLOSSARY

Bio – (biography) A condensed version of who

Direct Message or DM – this is like Twitter's internal e-mail system. When you send someone a direct message, it is private. No one can access the message except you and the person to whom you send it.

Followers – people who are following your account or updates on Twitter.

Hashtag – similar to a tag, a hashtag is a pound sign (#) followed by one or more words, which is used to categorize tweets. E.g. #writer.

Handle – your user name on Twitter.

Retweet (RT) – a message from someone else that you copy and send out on your timeline.

Tweeps or Tweeple – Twitter users who follow you.

Tweet – a message sent out using Twitter.

TweetIn – similar to a Twitter Chat (see below), except the tweeps meet in person at a set time to tweet.

Twitter Chat - online, public conversations that take place on Twitter at designated times around a unique hashtag.

Widget – software you can download and install to run a specific function on a website.

MORE RESOURCES AND INFORMATION

Links to Articles and Blog Posts

5 Tips for Writing Promoted Tweets That Drive Conversions
https://blog.hootsuite.com/how-to-increase-conversions-with-promoted-tweets/

7 Hilarious and Smart Twitter Bios to Check Out
https://blog.hootsuite.com/how-to-increase-conversions-with-promoted-tweets/

7 Simple Tips to Help You Promote Your Book on Twitter
http://blog.bookbaby.com/2013/01/promote-your-book-on-twitter-with-these-10-simple-tips/

10 Innovative Twitter Tools for the Busy Freelancer
http://www.designer-daily.com/10-innovative-twitter-tools-for-the-busy-freelancer-18460

10 Quick Tips to Easily Understand Twitter
https://blog.bufferapp.com/starting-out-on-twitter

10 Tips for Using Twitter to Grow Your Freelance Business
http://freelancefolder.com/10-tips-for-using-twitter-to-grow-your-freelance-business/

10 Types of Social Media Updates—How Many Are You Using?
http://michaelhyatt.com/10-types-of-social-media-updates.html

20+ Social Media Monitoring Tools for Business
http://www.digitalinformationworld.com/2015/03/the-20-best-social-media-monitoring-tools-infographic.html

40 Things to Tweet When Your Creativity Runs Dry
http://mixtusmedia.com/blog/40-things-to-tweet-when-your-creativity-runs-dry

100 Things to Tweet About on Twitter Besides Yourself
http://www.pammarketingnut.com/2013/03/100-things-to-tweet-about-on-twitter-besides-yourself/

100 Twitter Hashtags Every Writer Should Know
http://www.aerogrammestudio.com/2013/03/12/100-twitter-hashtags-every-writer-should-know/

100+ Twitter Tips for Businesses
http://www.digitalinformationworld.com/2013/08/8-infographics-100-twitter-tips-for-businesses.html

A Dr. Seuss Inspired Guide to Twitter
http://www.digitalinformationworld.com/2014/03/a-dr-seuss-guide-to-twitter-infographic.html

A Writers' Guide to Getting the Most Out of Twitter
http://michellerafter.com/2013/06/09/a-writers-guide-to-getting-the-most-out-of-twitter/

The Anatomy of a Flawless Social Media Post
http://twittercounter.com/blog/2015/05/the-anatomy-of-a-flawless-social-media-post/

Group Direct Messages and Mobile Video Camera
https://blog.twitter.com/2015/now-on-twitter-group-direct-messages-and-mobile-video-capture

Grow a Highly Targeted Twitter Following With This Trick
http://dustn.tv/targeted-twitter-followers/
How to Get 1,000 Followers on Twitter Tip Sheet
http://www.createyourself.com/wp-

content/uploads/1000+TwitterTipSheet.pdf

How to Optimize Your Twitter Bio to Gain More Followers
http://www.socialmediatoday.com/content/how-optimize-your-twitter-bio-gain-more-followers

The History and Power of Hashtags in Social Media Marketing
http://www.business2community.com/infographics/history-power-hashtags-social-media-marketing-infographic-0997768#KWIZalBmAjrD7KoV.97

How to Build Your Twitter Following with Raving Fans for Profit
http://www.matthewwoodward.co.uk/tutorials/create-raving-twitter-fans/

How to Get 1,000+ Followers on Twitter (Free Download)
http://offers.hubspot.com/grow-your-twitter-followers-fast

How to Get Noticed on Twitter – 15 Tips for Writers
http://www.makealivingwriting.com/writers-win-social-media/

How to Kick Off More Conversations on Twitter
https://blog.bufferapp.com/twitter-conversations

How to Send Group Direct Messages in Twitter on the iPhone
http://www.gottabemobile.com/2015/01/30/how-to-send-group-direct-messages-in-twitter-on-the-iphone/

How to Tweet on Twitter: 12 Templates to Get You Started
http://blog.hubspot.com/marketing/tweet-formulas-to-get-you-started-on-twitter#sm.001tmvneaclqf2a10bs1lrojpvgad

How to Twitter http://www.amazinginfographics.com/how-to-use-twitter-for-beginners/

How to Use Hashtags on Twitter: A Simple Guide for Marketers
http://blog.hubspot.com/blog/tabid/6307/bid/32497/How-to-Use-Hashtags-on-Twitter-A-Simple-Guide-for-Marketers.aspx

How to Use Twitter Like Margaret Atwood: Social Media Advice for Writers http://blog.bookbaby.com/2012/08/how-to-use-twitter-like-margaret-atwood-social-media-advice-for-authorspoets/
How to Write Catchy Headlines http://goinswriter.com/catchy-headlines/

My Twittonary: Every Twitter Term and Tool I Can Find
http://seedtheweb.com/2008/10/my-twittonary-every-twitter-term-and-tool-i-can-find/

The Best Twitter Widget (Tint) http://www.tintup.com/blog/the-best-twitter-widget/

The Science of Twitter (free chapter) http://offers.hubspot.com/the-science-of-twitter-free-chapter-download

Twitter brings live-streaming app Periscope to Android
http://www.theverge.com/2015/5/26/8657349/periscope-android-twitter

Twitter Launches Official WordPress Plugin
http://www.adweek.com/socialtimes/twitter-wordpress-plugin/615986

Twitter Manners http://inspiredm.com/exclusive-cheat-sheet-twitter-manners/

Twitter Marketing Tips for Freelance Writers
http://www.freelancewriting.com/top10tips/twitter-marketing-tips-for-freelance-writers.php

Twitterspeak: 66 Twitter Terms
http://mashable.com/2008/11/15/twitterspeak/

Twitter Streaming Library Built on Tweepy Enables Dynamic Term Tracking https://pypi.python.org/pypi/twitter-monitor/0.2.4

What is a Marketing Platform? http://www.platformpundit.com/what-is-a-marketing-platform/

Writing Good Tweets is More Art Than Science
http://personalweb.about.com/od/tweettips/a/Writing-Good-Tweets.htm

RECOMMENDED BOOKS

Denim, Amy *The Coffee Break Guide to Social Media for Writers: How to Succeed on Social Media and Still Have Time to Write.* (Nov. 13, 2013)

Flynn, Kathi *How to Tweet, The Basics: Dos and Don'ts for Newbies (Using Twitter)*

Hall, Rayne *Twitter for Writers (Writer's Craft).* *(June 6, 2014)*

Hegman, Sonja. *Moving at the Speed of Twitter: How Authors Can Build an Online Platform to Sell More books.* (Jan 6, 2014)

Hyatt, Michael. *Platform: Get Noticed in a Noisy World – A Step by Step Guide for Anyone with Something to Say or Sell.* *(2012)*

Kawala, Mike & David Boutin. *Twitter Marketing That Sells: How to Convert Your Twitter Followers into Business Dollars.* *(2016)*

McGraw, Danielle. *The Freelance Writer's Guide to Twitter Marketing.* (Dec. 1, 2012)

Nipps, Jen. *Get Twitter-pated: A Writer's Handbook to Twitter.* (March 24, 2012)

ABOUT THE AUTHOR

Ruth L. Snyder was privileged to spend the first 10 years of her life in southern Africa where her parents served as missionaries. From there her family moved to Canada, settling in Three Hills, Alberta. Ruth enjoyed her years as a "staff kid" at Prairie Bible College and is grateful for the biblical grounding she received there. She now resides close to Glendon (the pyrogy capital of Alberta, Canada) with her husband and five young children. Ruth enjoys writing articles, devotionals, short stories, and Christian fiction. She is author of *Cecile's Christmas Miracle*, *Life Lessons*, *Shadows and Sunshine*, and *Uplifting Devotionals for Parents*.

Ruth is a member of The Word Guild and The Christian PEN. She currently serves as the President of InScribe Christian Writers' Fellowship.

Ruth's children have taught her many things about living with special needs. She is a strong advocate who spent several years serving on her local public school board.

Ruth loves her job teaching Music for Young Children. She is fascinated by children's imaginations and enjoys helping young children learn the basics of music through play.

In her spare time, Ruth enjoys reading, crafts, volunteering in her local community, photography, and travel. Several years ago, Ruth and her family traveled through 28 States in 30 days!